Foreword

We live in an age of rapid innovation, where AI is no longer a futuristic concept confined to science fiction, but a practical tool we can all use in our daily lives. The power to simplify tasks, boost creativity, and streamline productivity is now at our fingertips, thanks to the rise of AI-driven tools. However, like any powerful tool, the real magic happens when we learn how to use it effectively—and that begins with knowing how to ask the right questions.

In this book, Beginners Guide to AI Prompts: Everyday Use for Everyone, you'll discover a practical, approachable, and engaging way to harness AI for everyday tasks. Whether you're writing emails, managing your budget, planning meals, or improving your productivity, this guide breaks down how to craft effective prompts to get the most out of AI tools. It doesn't matter if you're a tech enthusiast or someone who has never used AI before—this book is designed to meet you where you are and give you confidence in your AI journey.

What sets this guide apart is its focus on real-world applications. It's not just about understanding AI concepts; it's about learning how AI can genuinely improve your life. The chapters are packed with practical examples, useful tips, and easy-to-follow prompts that make AI accessible, fun, and effective.

But beyond the utility, this book emphasizes ethical and responsible AI use. As we embrace these new technologies, it's crucial to use them wisely, thoughtfully, and with a sense of responsibility. The reminders to verify information, respect privacy, and give credit where it's due are more important now than ever.

The future of AI is collaborative—humans and AI working together to solve problems, inspire ideas, and create a better, more efficient world. This book gives you the tools to be part of that future. You'll learn not just to use AI, but to partner with AI, enhancing your abilities and expanding your potential.

So, as you turn the pages and start experimenting with the prompts, remember: the possibilities are endless, and the power is in your hands. Whether you're automating tasks, brainstorming ideas, or just exploring AI out of curiosity, the journey ahead is exciting.

Let this book be your guide as you step into a world where AI is your ally, and every prompt you write is a step toward discovery, efficiency, and creativity.

Happy prompting!

Table of Contents

1. Introduction to AI Prompts
2. Crafting Effective Prompts: Best Practices
3. Prompts for Writing Emails
4. Prompts for Educational Purposes
5. Ethical and Responsible AI Use
6. Prompts for Social Media Posts
7. Prompts for Spreadsheets and Data Tasks
8. Prompts for Personal Finance Management
9. Prompts for Recipes and Meal Planning
10. Prompts for Time Management and Productivity
11. Advanced Prompting Tips
12. FAQs and Common Pitfalls
13. Conclusion and Next Steps

Chapter 1: Introduction to AI Prompts

What is a Prompt?

A **prompt** is the instruction or question you give to an AI tool to generate a response or perform a task. Think of it like giving directions to a helpful assistant. The clearer your instructions, the better the output you receive.

At its core, a prompt can be as simple as a question or as detailed as a step-by-step request. For example:

- **Simple Prompt**: "Give me a motivational quote."
- **Detailed Prompt**: "Write a motivational quote that encourages perseverance in difficult times."

The more specific you are, the closer the AI's response will match your needs.

Why Use AI Prompts in Daily Life?

AI prompts aren't just for tech enthusiasts—they're tools that everyone can use to simplify and enhance their daily tasks. Here are some key benefits of using AI prompts:

1. Efficiency

Save Time on Everyday Tasks: AI can quickly generate emails, meal plans, schedules, or summaries. Instead of spending hours drafting content or organizing tasks, a well-crafted prompt can give you what you need in seconds.

Example Prompt:
"Write a professional follow-up email thanking a client for their time and confirming our next meeting."

2. Creativity

Brainstorm New Ideas: Whether you're stuck on what to post on social media or need fresh ideas for a project, AI can help spark creativity. Use prompts to explore different perspectives or styles.

Example Prompt:
"Give me five blog post ideas about sustainable living for beginners."

3. Productivity

Streamline Daily Routines: From managing finances to planning meals, AI prompts can help you stay organized and productive. They can help you create schedules, track goals, or set reminders.

Example Prompt:
"Create a weekly meal plan that includes quick, healthy dinners."

4. Accessibility

No Technical Skills Required: You don't need to be a tech expert to use AI prompts. If you can write a simple question or request, you can use AI to assist with tasks. This makes AI an accessible tool for people of all backgrounds and skill levels.

Example Prompt:
"Explain the basics of investing to someone who's never done it before."

How Do AI Prompts Fit into Your Life?

AI prompts can become a valuable tool in many areas of your life:

- **At Work**: Draft emails, create reports, or generate ideas for presentations.
- **At School**: Summarize articles, generate study guides, or practice quizzes.
- **At Home**: Plan meals, organize your budget, or manage your time.
- **On Social Media**: Write engaging posts, captions, or hashtags to connect with others.

With a little practice, you'll discover how versatile and helpful AI prompts can be!

By the end of this book, you'll have a toolkit of practical prompts to make your everyday tasks simpler, faster, and more creative. Let's dive in!

Chapter 2: Crafting Effective Prompts

Now that you know what a prompt is and how it can help you in everyday tasks, it's time to learn how to **craft effective prompts**. The quality of the AI's output depends largely on the instructions you give. Think of your prompt as a guide—the clearer and more detailed it is, the better the results will be.

Here are some key tips for writing great prompts that will help you get exactly what you're looking for.

Tips for Writing Great Prompts

1. Be Specific

When you're too vague, the AI might produce content that doesn't match your expectations. Adding specific details helps the AI understand exactly what you want.

Example:
✗ *"Write a post."*

■ *"Write a friendly LinkedIn post about the importance of teamwork in a remote work environment."*

The second prompt gives clear instructions about the **tone** (friendly), **platform** (LinkedIn), and **topic** (teamwork in remote work). The more specific you are, the closer the AI will get to your desired outcome.

---

2. Include Context

Providing background information helps the AI tailor its response to your needs. Think of it like giving a friend context before asking for advice—they'll give better suggestions when they understand the situation.

Example:
✗ *"Write a thank-you email."*
■ *"Write a thank-you email to a colleague who helped me finish a big project on time. Mention how their support made a difference and express my gratitude for their hard work."*

By adding context (colleague, big project, timely completion), the AI can create a more personalized and meaningful email.

---

3. Set the Tone

Specifying the tone helps ensure the AI's response matches the mood you're aiming for. Do you want the response to be **casual, professional, humorous, motivational, or formal**? Including tone instructions helps refine the output.

Example:
✗ *"Write a message about our company's anniversary."*
■ *"Write a cheerful and celebratory message for our company's 10th anniversary to share on social media."*

By stating that you want a **cheerful and celebratory tone**, the AI knows how to style the message appropriately.

---

4. Iterate and Refine

Don't worry if your first prompt doesn't yield the perfect result. AI responses can often improve with a little tweaking. If the output isn't quite right, adjust your prompt by adding more detail or clarifying your instructions.

Example:

- **Initial Prompt**: "Write a blog post about time management."
- **Result**: The response is too general and lacks motivation.

- **Refined Prompt**: "Write a 500-word blog post about the importance of time management, using a motivational and encouraging tone, and include practical tips for beginners."

Each iteration helps you fine-tune the AI's response until it meets your needs.

Putting It All Together

Here's a quick summary of the key tips:

1. **Be Specific**: Clearly state what you want.
2. **Include Context**: Give background details to provide clarity.
3. **Set the Tone**: Define the mood or style you're aiming for.
4. **Iterate**: Adjust your prompt based on the AI's output.

Example of an Effective Prompt:

■ *"Create a 5-tweet thread explaining the benefits of using AI in daily life, written in an informative and upbeat tone, and suitable for beginners."*

This prompt is specific (5-tweet thread), includes context (benefits of AI in daily life), sets the tone (informative and upbeat), and clarifies the audience (beginners).

With these strategies, you'll be able to craft prompts that help you get exactly what you need from AI. In the following chapters, you'll see how these principles apply to specific tasks like writing emails, managing finances, and more!

Chapter 3: Prompts for Writing Emails

Writing emails is a daily task for most of us, whether for work, school, or personal matters. Crafting the perfect email can be time-consuming, but AI can help you create clear, professional, and effective messages in seconds. In this chapter, you'll find practical prompts for different types of emails to streamline your communication.

Common Use Cases for AI-Generated Emails

1. Professional Emails

Whether you're reaching out to clients, managers, or colleagues, professional emails need to be clear, courteous, and concise.

Prompt Example:
"Draft a professional email requesting a meeting with a client to discuss next quarter's goals."

AI Response Example:

Subject: Request for Meeting to Discuss Next Quarter's Goals

Dear [Client's Name],

I hope this email finds you well. As we approach the end of this quarter, I'd love the opportunity to meet and discuss our goals for the next quarter. I believe a focused discussion will help us align our strategies and ensure we're on track to meet our objectives.

Would you be available for a 30-minute meeting sometime next week? I'm happy to accommodate your schedule.

Thank you for your time and consideration. I look forward to hearing from you soon.

Best regards,
[Your Name]
[Your Position]
[Your Company]

_____
_____

2. Polite Follow-Up Emails

Sometimes, people need a gentle reminder. A polite follow-up email helps keep things on track without seeming pushy or rude.

Prompt Example:
"Write a polite follow-up email reminding a colleague to submit their part of a project."

AI Response Example:

Subject: Quick Reminder: Project Submission Due

Hi [Colleague's Name],

I hope you're doing well. I just wanted to gently remind you that the deadline for your part of the [Project Name] is coming up on [Due Date]. Your contribution is essential for us to move forward, and I really appreciate all the work you've put into it so far.

Please let me know if there's anything you need or if you're facing any challenges—I'm happy to help.

Thanks again, and looking forward to your submission!

Best,
[Your Name]

3. Apology Emails

Mistakes happen, but a sincere and well-crafted apology can go a long way in maintaining trust.

Prompt Example:
"Compose an apologetic email to a customer whose order was delayed."

AI Response Example:

Subject: Our Sincere Apologies for Your Delayed Order

Dear [Customer's Name],

I want to sincerely apologize for the delay in delivering your recent order [Order Number]. We know how important it is to receive your items on time, and we're truly sorry for falling short of your expectations.

The delay was caused by [brief explanation, e.g., unexpected shipping issues], and we are taking steps to ensure this doesn't happen again. Your order is now on its way and is expected to arrive by [New Delivery Date].

To make up for this inconvenience, we'd like to offer you [a discount, a gift card, free shipping on your next order, etc.]. We appreciate your patience and understanding, and we hope to continue serving you in the future.

If you have any questions or concerns, please don't hesitate to reach out to us at [Contact Information].

Warm regards,
[Your Name]
[Your Position]
[Company Name]

Other Useful Email Scenarios

Here are a few more common email prompts you can try:

1. **Request for Information**:
   Prompt: "Write an email asking a vendor for details about their new product line."

2. **Thank You Email**:
   Prompt: "Compose a thank-you email to a mentor for their career advice and support."
3. **Invitation Email**:
   Prompt: "Draft an invitation email for a team-building event scheduled next month."
4. **Job Application Email**:
   Prompt: "Write an email to accompany a job application for a marketing coordinator position."

Tips for Effective Email Prompts

1. **Include the Purpose**: Clearly state what the email is for (e.g., follow-up, request, apology).
2. **Add Recipient Details**: Specify the type of recipient (client, colleague, customer) to help the AI set the appropriate tone.
3. **Mention Key Points**: Include important details like deadlines, reasons for the email, or desired outcomes.
4. **Tone**: Indicate whether you want the email to be professional, friendly, apologetic, or persuasive.

Example of a Detailed Prompt:
"Write a professional but friendly email to a client apologizing for a missed deadline and offering a solution to complete the project."

By using these prompts and tips, you'll be able to write emails that are effective, clear, and perfectly suited to your needs. In the next chapter, we'll explore how AI can help with educational tasks and learning!

Chapter 4: Prompts for Educational Purposes

AI tools can be incredibly useful for students, parents, and teachers. From helping with homework to explaining difficult concepts or generating practice quizzes, AI can make learning more accessible and engaging. In this chapter, you'll find practical prompts to assist with various educational tasks, including summarizing notes, learning new topics, and creating quizzes. These prompts are designed to provide clear, accurate, and age-appropriate information.

Homework and Study Aids

1. Summarizing Notes

Summaries help students focus on key information without getting overwhelmed. AI can quickly condense lengthy material into easy-to-understand summaries tailored to different grade levels.

Prompt Example:

"Summarize the key points from the water cycle for a 5th-grade science student."

AI Response Example:

The Water Cycle Summary for 5th Graders

The water cycle is how water moves around Earth. It has a few main steps:

1. **Evaporation**: When the sun heats water in rivers, lakes, or oceans, the water turns into a gas called vapor and rises into the air.
2. **Condensation**: As the vapor rises, it cools down and turns back into tiny water droplets, forming clouds.
3. **Precipitation**: When the clouds get full of water, the water falls back to Earth as rain, snow, or hail.
4. **Collection**: The water collects in rivers, lakes, and oceans, and the cycle starts again.

This cycle keeps water moving all around the planet!

---

2. Learning New Topics

AI can break down complex topics into simple explanations for different learning levels. This is particularly useful when students need extra help understanding a new concept.

Prompt Example:
"Explain the basics of photosynthesis in simple terms for a middle school student."

AI Response Example:

Photosynthesis Explained for Middle Schoolers

Photosynthesis is the way plants make their food. Here's how it works:

1. **Sunlight**: Plants use energy from the sun.
2. **Leaves**: The leaves take in a gas called carbon dioxide (CO_2) from the air.
3. **Roots**: The roots absorb water (H_2O) from the soil.
4. **Chlorophyll**: Inside the leaves, a green chemical called chlorophyll uses sunlight to turn carbon dioxide and water into **glucose** (a type of sugar) and **oxygen**.

The plant uses the glucose for energy to grow, and the oxygen is released back into the air. This process helps plants survive and gives us the oxygen we need to breathe!

---

3. Practice Quizzes

Quizzes are a great way to test knowledge and reinforce learning. With AI, you can quickly create customized quizzes on any subject.

Prompt Example:
"Create a 5-question multiple-choice quiz on the American Revolution."

AI Response Example:

Quiz on the American Revolution

1. **What year did the American Revolution begin?**
    a) 1750
    b) 1775
    c) 1789
    d) 1800
    Answer: b) 1775
2. **Which event is known as the start of the American Revolution?**
    a) The Boston Tea Party
    b) The Declaration of Independence
    c) The Battles of Lexington and Concord

d) The signing of the Constitution
   Answer: c) The Battles of Lexington and Concord
3. **Who wrote the Declaration of Independence?**
   a) George Washington
   b) Thomas Jefferson
   c) Benjamin Franklin
   d) John Adams
   Answer: b) Thomas Jefferson
4. **What was the main reason the colonies wanted independence?**
   a) To explore new lands
   b) To gain freedom from British taxes and control
   c) To form a stronger government
   d) To end slavery
   Answer: b) To gain freedom from British taxes and control
5. **Which treaty ended the American Revolution?**
   a) Treaty of Paris (1783)
   b) Treaty of Versailles
   c) Treaty of Ghent
   d) Treaty of London
   Answer: a) Treaty of Paris (1783)

Other Educational Use Cases

Here are additional scenarios where AI prompts can support learning:

1. **Essay Outlines**:
   Prompt: "Create a 3-point outline for an essay about the benefits of recycling."
2. **Definitions**:
   Prompt: "Define the term 'ecosystem' in a way that a 6th-grade student can understand."
3. **Study Plans**:
   Prompt: "Create a 2-week study plan for preparing for a math exam."
4. **Historical Timelines**:
   Prompt: "Create a timeline of key events during the Civil Rights Movement."

Tips for Educational Prompts

1. **Specify the Grade Level**: This helps the AI adjust the complexity of the language.
2. **Clarify the Topic**: Include key details about what you need explained or summarized.
3. **Set the Format**: Mention if you need a summary, list, quiz, or essay outline.

4. **Indicate the Length**: If needed, state how long you want the response to be (e.g., "a 100-word summary").

Example of a Detailed Prompt:
"Summarize the causes of World War II in 150 words for a high school history student."

By using these prompts, students and educators can simplify learning, make studying more interactive, and get the support they need to succeed. In the next chapter, we'll explore how to use AI responsibly and ethically!

Chapter 5: Ethical and Responsible AI Use

As AI becomes a part of everyday life, it's important to use it ethically and responsibly. While AI can be a powerful tool for productivity and creativity, misuse can lead to unintended consequences like spreading misinformation, violating privacy, or failing to acknowledge AI's contributions. This chapter outlines best practices to help you use AI tools in a way that's fair, safe, and transparent.

Best Practices for Ethical AI Use

1. Give Credit

When AI assists you in creating content, it's good practice to let others know. This transparency helps set clear expectations and promotes honesty. Whether you're writing blog posts, articles, or school assignments, acknowledging AI contributions respects the work of both humans and technology.

How to Give Credit:

- **In Articles or Blog Posts**: Add a note like, "This piece was created with the assistance of AI."
- **For Educational Assignments**: Mention, "Portions of this research summary were generated using AI tools."
- **On Social Media**: Use hashtags like #AIAssisted or #CreatedWithAI.

Example Statement:
"This guide was drafted using AI-generated prompts and refined with human editing."

Why It Matters:

- Builds trust with your audience.
- Helps others understand how AI can support creativity.
- Avoids misrepresenting AI-generated work as entirely human-made.

---

2. Avoid Misinformation

AI tools are powerful, but they are not perfect. They can sometimes generate content that is inaccurate or outdated. Always double-check the facts, especially when creating content for educational, professional, or public purposes.

Best Practices for Fact-Checking AI Outputs:

- **Cross-Check Sources**: Verify information using reliable websites, books, or trusted experts.
- **Check Dates**: AI may not have access to the latest information, so confirm dates and recent events.
- **Watch Out for Biases**: AI models can reflect biases in the data they were trained on. Stay critical of potentially one-sided or misleading information.

Example Scenario:
Prompt: "Write a summary of recent climate change events."
Best Practice: After receiving the AI's response, check reputable sources (like NASA or the World Meteorological Organization) to confirm accuracy before sharing.

Why It Matters:

- Prevents spreading false or misleading information.
- Promotes reliable knowledge sharing.
- Helps maintain your credibility.

---

3. Respect Privacy

When using AI tools, avoid including personal, sensitive, or confidential information in your prompts. AI systems process the data you provide, and while many are designed with privacy safeguards, it's best to err on the side of caution.

Information to Avoid in Prompts:

- **Personal Identifiers**: Full names, addresses, phone numbers, or Social Security numbers.
- **Confidential Data**: Business secrets, private work documents, or financial information.
- **Sensitive Topics**: Information about health, relationships, or legal matters.

Safe Prompt Example:
"Draft a professional email to a client to schedule a meeting."

Unsafe Prompt Example:
"Draft a professional email to my client John Smith at 123 Main St. about his recent loan application."

Why It Matters:

- Protects your privacy and the privacy of others.
- Reduces the risk of data breaches or misuse.
- Maintains confidentiality in professional settings.

Other Ethical Considerations

1. Use AI to Empower, Not Exploit

AI should be used to support creativity, learning, and productivity, not to deceive or manipulate. Avoid using AI to create fake news, plagiarized content, or misleading social media posts.

2. Be Transparent About Limitations

Let others know that AI has limitations. AI-generated content is a tool, but human judgment is still essential for context, accuracy, and empathy.

3. Encourage AI Literacy

Help others understand how AI works and how to use it responsibly. Promoting AI literacy ensures more people can benefit from AI while recognizing its potential pitfalls.

Summary of Ethical Guidelines

1. **Give Credit**: Acknowledge AI's role in content creation.
2. **Avoid Misinformation**: Always verify AI-generated facts before sharing.
3. **Respect Privacy**: Don't include sensitive information in prompts.
4. **Use AI to Empower**: Ensure your use of AI promotes honesty and fairness.

5. **Be Transparent**: Make others aware of AI's strengths and limitations.

By following these best practices, you can ensure that your use of AI is ethical, responsible, and beneficial to both you and the people around you. In the next chapter, we'll explore prompts for creating engaging and effective social media posts!

Chapter 6: Prompts for Social Media Posts

In today's digital world, social media is a key tool for connecting, sharing, and building your personal or professional brand. Crafting engaging and relevant content can help you stand out, and AI can assist you in generating posts, captions, and hashtags that capture attention and drive interaction. Whether you're sharing a stunning photo on Instagram, offering professional insights on LinkedIn, or looking for the perfect hashtags to boost your reach, these prompts will make content creation easier and more effective.

Craft Engaging Content

1. Instagram Caption

Instagram thrives on visuals, but a great caption can enhance your post by adding personality, context, or humor. AI can help generate captions that match the tone and vibe of your image.

Prompt Example:
"Write a fun and witty caption for a beach sunset photo."

AI Response Example:

"Chasing sunsets and dreams 🌅✨ Because some things are just too beautiful to let slip away! #BeachVibes #SunsetLover"

Variation:
"Sea you at sunset! 🌊💥 Who else thinks the ocean and sunsets are the ultimate power couple? #OceanMagic #GoldenHour"

---

2. LinkedIn Post

LinkedIn is the place for professional insights, career stories, and industry updates. Thoughtful and well-crafted posts can spark discussions and build your network. AI can help you write posts that are professional, insightful, and engaging.

Prompt Example:
"Create a thoughtful LinkedIn post about the importance of mentorship in career growth."

AI Response Example:

Mentorship: The Key to Unlocking Career Potential

In my career journey, I've come to realize the incredible value of having a mentor. A mentor offers guidance, shares experiences, and pushes you to reach your full potential. One piece of advice from my mentor that stuck with me is: *"Growth happens just outside your comfort zone."*

Through mentorship, I've gained confidence to take on challenges I once thought were beyond me. I believe that having someone to guide and support you is one of the most powerful ways to grow professionally.

If you've had a mentor who helped shape your career, take a moment to thank them today. And if you have the chance to mentor someone, embrace it—you might change their career path for the better!

I'd love to hear: How has mentorship impacted your career? Share your experiences in the comments!

#CareerGrowth #Mentorship #ProfessionalDevelopment

---

3. Hashtag Suggestions

Hashtags are crucial for making your posts discoverable to a wider audience. The right hashtags can improve your reach and engagement. AI can help generate relevant and trending hashtags for your posts.

Prompt Example:
"Suggest 5 hashtags for a post about homemade recipes."

AI Response Example:

1. **#HomeCookedMeals**
2. **#EasyRecipes**
3. **#FoodLovers**
4. **#MadeFromScratch**
5. **#TastyAtHome**

Other Types of Social Media Prompts

1. Facebook Status Update

Prompt Example:
"Write a heartfelt Facebook post about adopting a new pet."

AI Response Example:

"Meet [Pet's Name], the newest (and furriest) member of our family! 🐾🖤 We couldn't be happier to give this little one a loving home. Already, [he/she/they] has filled our lives with joy, laughter, and a few chewed-up shoes! If you're thinking about adopting, do it—you might just meet your new best friend. #AdoptDontShop #NewFamilyMember"

---

2. Twitter/X Post (Tweet)

Prompt Example:
"Write a motivational tweet about staying productive during the week."

AI Response Example:

"Every Monday is a fresh start. Set your goals, chase them down, and make this week count! 💪 #MotivationMonday #ProductivityTips"

---

3. YouTube Video Description

Prompt Example:
"Write a YouTube video description for a baking tutorial on making chocolate chip cookies."

AI Response Example:

Title: *"The BEST Chocolate Chip Cookie Recipe – Easy and Delicious!"*

Description:
Ready to bake the perfect chocolate chip cookies? 🍪 In this video, I'll show you step-by-step how to make soft, chewy cookies with just the right amount of chocolate chips. Perfect for beginners or anyone craving a classic treat! Don't forget to like, comment, and subscribe for more yummy recipes. Happy baking!

#BakingTutorial #ChocolateChipCookies #EasyRecipes

Tips for Effective Social Media Prompts

1. **Know Your Platform**: Tailor your tone and content to the platform you're using. LinkedIn posts are professional, while Instagram captions can be more playful.
2. **Set the Tone**: Specify if you want the content to be fun, inspirational, informative, or persuasive.
3. **Add Details**: Including context like the type of image, topic, or audience will help the AI generate more relevant content.
4. **Engage Your Audience**: Encourage interaction by asking a question or inviting comments.

Detailed Prompt Example:
"Write an engaging Instagram caption for a photo of a homemade pizza, focusing on the joy of cooking with family."

By using these prompts, you'll be able to create social media content that is engaging, relevant, and tailored to your audience. In the next chapter, we'll explore prompts for managing spreadsheets and data tasks!

Chapter 7: Prompts for Spreadsheets and Data Tasks

Spreadsheets are powerful tools for organizing, analyzing, and managing data, but creating them from scratch can sometimes feel overwhelming. With AI, you can generate prompts to automate data tasks, create templates, and organize information effortlessly. Whether you're keeping track of your expenses, building a budget, or managing data for work, these prompts can save time and streamline your workflow.

Automating Data Organization

AI can help structure your data more efficiently by creating categories, templates, and lists. Here are some practical prompts to get your spreadsheets in order.

1. Organize Expenses

Tracking your expenses is essential for managing personal finances or running a small business. With the right categories, you can see where your money is going and identify areas where you can save.

Prompt Example:
"Generate categories to organize monthly expenses in a spreadsheet."

AI Response Example:

Here are categories to help organize your monthly expenses:

Category	Examples
Housing	Rent, Mortgage, Property Taxes, Insurance
Utilities	Electricity, Water, Internet, Gas, Trash
Transportation	Gas, Public Transport, Car Payments, Maintenance
Groceries	Supermarket, Farmers' Market, Bulk Items
Dining Out	Restaurants, Takeout, Coffee Shops

Healthcare	Doctor Visits, Medications, Insurance Premiums
Personal Care	Haircuts, Skincare, Gym Memberships
Entertainment	Movies, Streaming Services, Concerts
Debt Payments	Credit Card, Loans
Savings/Investments	Emergency Fund, Retirement, Investments
Miscellaneous	Gifts, Donations, Shopping, Hobbies

You can use these categories as column headers in your spreadsheet to track each expense efficiently.

---

2. Create a Budget Template

A budget helps you plan your income, expenses, and savings. AI can generate a simple template to keep your finances organized and help you stay on track.

Prompt Example:
"Design a simple budget spreadsheet for tracking income and expenses."

AI Response Example:

Category	Planned Amount	Actual Amount	Difference
Income			
- Salary	$	$	$
- Freelance/Side Income	$	$	$
Expenses			
- Housing	$	$	$
- Utilities	$	$	$
- Groceries	$	$	$
- Transportation	$	$	$
- Healthcare	$	$	$
- Entertainment	$	$	$
- Miscellaneous	$	$	$
Savings/Investments	$	$	$
Total	$	$	$

Instructions:

1. **Planned Amount**: Enter your expected income and expenses for the month.
2. **Actual Amount**: Record the actual amounts as they occur.
3. **Difference**: Calculate the difference by subtracting the actual amount from the planned amount. This helps you see if you're over or under budget.

Other Useful Prompts for Data Tasks

1. Create a To-Do List Tracker

Prompt: "Design a spreadsheet to track daily tasks with columns for task description, priority, status, and due date."

AI Response Example:

Task	Priority	Status	Due Date
Finish report	High	In Progress	July 15
Schedule team meeting	Medium	Not Started	July 18
Buy groceries	Low	Completed	July 12

2. Track Project Deadlines

Prompt: "Create a project tracking spreadsheet with columns for task name, assigned person, deadline, and progress."

AI Response Example:

Task Name	Assigned To	Deadline	Progress
Design website layout	Alex	August 5	50% Complete
Write blog post	Jamie	August 8	Not Started
Conduct user testing	Morgan	August 15	10% Complete

3. Inventory Management

Prompt: "Generate a basic inventory spreadsheet with columns for item name, quantity, supplier, and restock date."

AI Response Example:

Item Name	Quantity	Supplier	Restock Date
Printer Paper	500 sheets	Office Supplies Inc.	August 1
Ink Cartridges	20	PrintMasters Ltd.	July 20
Notebooks	100	Stationery World	August 10

Tips for Effective Spreadsheet Prompts

1. **Be Clear About the Purpose**: Specify what you want the spreadsheet to track (e.g., budget, tasks, inventory).
2. **List Key Columns**: Mention the headers you need (e.g., date, category, amount).
3. **Include Examples**: Providing sample data in your prompt helps the AI understand the format you want.
4. **Indicate Complexity**: Specify if you want a simple layout or more advanced features like formulas or charts.

Detailed Prompt Example:
"Design a budget spreadsheet with columns for income, expenses, planned amount, actual amount, and difference. Include formulas to calculate the total for each category."

By using these prompts, you can create organized, efficient, and user-friendly spreadsheets for a variety of tasks. In the next chapter, we'll explore how AI can help you manage your personal finances with ease!

Chapter 8: Prompts for Personal Finance Management

Managing your finances can feel overwhelming, but with the right tools and strategies, you can take control of your money and work toward your financial goals. AI can help simplify personal finance tasks like planning savings goals, understanding investments, and tracking spending. In this chapter, we'll explore how AI prompts can assist with creating savings plans and beginner-friendly investment strategies.

Financial Planning

Financial planning helps you manage your money effectively and achieve your short-term and long-term goals. AI can generate practical plans and offer advice tailored to your specific needs and resources.

1. Savings Goals

Setting clear, achievable savings goals is the first step to building financial security. Whether you're saving for an emergency fund, a vacation, or a new gadget, breaking it down into smaller milestones makes it more manageable.

Prompt Example:
"Create a 6-month savings plan to save $1,000 with weekly milestones."

AI Response Example:

6-Month Savings Plan to Save $1,000

To save $1,000 in 6 months (26 weeks), you need to break it down into weekly contributions. Here's a simple plan:

1. **Goal**: $1,000
2. **Duration**: 6 months (26 weeks)
3. **Weekly Savings Target**: $1,000 ÷ 26 weeks = **$38.50 per week**

Weekly Milestones:

Week	Total Saved	Weekly Contribution
1	$38.50	$38.50
2	$77.00	$38.50

3	$115.50	$38.50
4	$154.00	$38.50
...	...	...
26	$1,000	$38.50

Tips to Stay on Track:

1. **Automate Your Savings**: Set up a weekly automatic transfer to your savings account.
2. **Cut Unnecessary Expenses**: Skip a few coffee runs or pack lunch instead of eating out.
3. **Track Your Progress**: Review your milestones every month to stay motivated.

---

2. Investment Strategy

Investing can be an effective way to grow your wealth, but it can be intimidating if you're a beginner. AI can provide simple, beginner-friendly investment strategies to help you get started with a small amount of money.

Prompt Example:
"Explain a beginner-friendly investment strategy for someone starting with $500."

AI Response Example:

Beginner-Friendly Investment Strategy for $500

If you're new to investing and have $500 to start with, here's a straightforward strategy to help you grow your money over time:

1. **Step 1: Open an Investment Account**
   - Choose a **brokerage account** or a **robo-advisor** (like Betterment, Acorns, or Wealthfront). Robo-advisors are great for beginners because they automatically manage your investments based on your goals and risk level.
2. **Step 2: Invest in Exchange-Traded Funds (ETFs)**
   - ETFs are baskets of stocks or bonds that give you diversification (spreading your risk across multiple assets). They're affordable, easy to understand, and less risky than picking individual stocks.
   - Consider investing in a **broad market ETF** like:
     - **S&P 500 ETF** (e.g., VOO or SPY) for exposure to the top 500 U.S. companies.
     - **Total Stock Market ETF** (e.g., VTI) for exposure to the entire U.S. stock market.
3. **Step 3: Contribute Regularly**
   - Even if you start with $500, adding small amounts each month (e.g., $25 or $50) can help grow your investments faster through **dollar-cost averaging**

(investing a fixed amount regularly to reduce the impact of market volatility).
4. **Step 4: Think Long-Term**
    - Investing is most effective when you leave your money to grow over several years. Avoid withdrawing funds during short-term market drops.

Example Portfolio with $500:

- **50% ($250)** in a broad market ETF (e.g., S&P 500 ETF)
- **30% ($150)** in a bond ETF for stability (e.g., BND)
- **20% ($100)** in an international stock ETF (e.g., VXUS) for global diversification

Tips for New Investors:

- **Stay Informed**: Learn basic investing concepts through blogs, videos, or podcasts.
- **Avoid High Fees**: Choose low-cost ETFs to maximize returns.
- **Stay Patient**: Investing takes time. Focus on long-term growth instead of quick gains.

Other Useful Personal Finance Prompts

1. Debt Repayment Plan

Prompt: *"Create a 12-month debt repayment plan to pay off $3,000 in credit card debt with 18% interest."*

2. Emergency Fund Plan

Prompt: *"Outline a strategy to build a $2,000 emergency fund in 1 year."*

3. Retirement Planning

Prompt: *"Explain a simple retirement savings plan for someone who wants to start saving at age 30."*

4. Financial Goal Tracker

Prompt: *"Design a spreadsheet to track multiple financial goals like saving for a vacation, a car, and a new computer."*

Tips for Creating Effective Personal Finance Prompts

1. **Specify the Goal**: Be clear about what you want to achieve (e.g., saving $1,000, investing $500).
2. **Include a Timeline**: Adding a timeframe helps create realistic and structured plans.
3. **Define the Risk Level**: For investment prompts, specify if you want low-risk, moderate-risk, or high-risk strategies.
4. **Mention Constraints**: If you have budget limits or specific requirements, include those details in your prompt.

Example of a Detailed Prompt:
"Create a 3-month plan to save $600 for a weekend trip. I can contribute up to $50 per week, but I need suggestions for cutting expenses."

By using these AI-generated prompts, you can simplify personal finance management, create achievable goals, and build a stronger financial future. In the next chapter, we'll explore how AI can help with recipes and meal planning to make your daily life even more organized!

Chapter 9: Prompts for Recipes and Meal Planning

Cooking at home can save money, promote healthier eating habits, and be an enjoyable experience. However, planning meals and coming up with new recipe ideas can sometimes be a challenge. AI can simplify this by generating quick recipes, meal plans, and creative cooking ideas tailored to your needs. Whether you're looking for a speedy dinner option or a full weekly plan, AI prompts can help you stay organized and inspired in the kitchen.

Effortless Cooking Ideas

1. Quick Dinner Recipes

Sometimes, you need a nutritious meal in a hurry. With the right AI prompt, you can generate quick recipes that are easy to follow and use common ingredients.

Prompt Example:
"Give me a 20-minute vegetarian dinner recipe with pasta and vegetables."

AI Response Example:

Quick 20-Minute Veggie Pasta

Ingredients:

- 8 oz (225g) spaghetti or any pasta of your choice
- 2 tbsp olive oil
- 2 cloves garlic, minced
- 1 small onion, diced
- 1 bell pepper, chopped
- 1 zucchini, sliced
- 1 cup cherry tomatoes, halved
- 2 cups fresh spinach
- 1/2 tsp dried oregano
- Salt and pepper to taste
- Grated Parmesan (optional)

Instructions:

1. **Cook the pasta**: Boil a pot of salted water. Add the pasta and cook according to the package instructions (about 8-10 minutes). Reserve 1/2 cup of pasta water, then drain the pasta.
2. **Sauté the veggies**: In a large pan, heat olive oil over medium heat. Add garlic and onion and sauté for 2 minutes. Add bell pepper and zucchini, and cook for another 5 minutes.

3. **Add tomatoes and spinach**: Stir in cherry tomatoes and cook for 2 minutes until softened. Add spinach and let it wilt.
4. **Combine with pasta**: Add the cooked pasta to the pan. Toss everything together, adding a bit of the reserved pasta water if needed. Season with oregano, salt, and pepper.
5. **Serve**: Top with grated Parmesan if desired and serve warm.

Time: 20 minutes
Serves: 2-3

---

2. Weekly Meal Plan

Planning meals for the week helps reduce stress, minimize food waste, and ensure you have balanced, nutritious options ready to go. AI can generate meal plans tailored to your dietary preferences and time constraints.

Prompt Example:
"Create a healthy 5-day meal plan with easy-to-cook recipes."

AI Response Example:

5-Day Healthy Meal Plan

Day 1: Monday

- **Breakfast**: Greek yogurt with honey, fresh berries, and granola.
- **Lunch**: Grilled chicken Caesar salad with whole-grain croutons.
- **Dinner**: Baked salmon with roasted sweet potatoes and steamed broccoli.

Day 2: Tuesday

- **Breakfast**: Overnight oats with banana, chia seeds, and almond butter.
- **Lunch**: Turkey and avocado wrap with baby carrots.
- **Dinner**: Stir-fried tofu and mixed vegetables with brown rice.

Day 3: Wednesday

- **Breakfast**: Smoothie with spinach, pineapple, banana, and protein powder.
- **Lunch**: Quinoa salad with chickpeas, cherry tomatoes, cucumber, and lemon-tahini dressing.
- **Dinner**: Shrimp fajitas with bell peppers, onions, and whole-wheat tortillas.

Day 4: Thursday

- **Breakfast**: Scrambled eggs with sautéed spinach and whole-grain toast.
- **Lunch**: Lentil soup with a side of mixed greens.
- **Dinner**: Grilled chicken with mashed cauliflower and green beans.

Day 5: Friday

- **Breakfast**: Cottage cheese with sliced peaches and walnuts.
- **Lunch**: Tuna salad stuffed into a whole-grain pita.
- **Dinner**: Spaghetti with turkey meatballs and a side of steamed broccoli.

Tips for the Week:

- **Prep Ahead**: Chop vegetables, cook grains, and marinate proteins in advance to save time.
- **Flexible Swaps**: Swap proteins (e.g., chicken for tofu) or sides (e.g., rice for quinoa) to fit your taste and dietary needs.

Other Useful Recipe and Meal Planning Prompts

1. Meal Prep Ideas for the Week

Prompt:
"Suggest 3 easy meal prep recipes that I can make on Sunday for the workweek."

2. Healthy Snack Ideas

Prompt:
"Give me 5 healthy snack ideas that don't require cooking."

AI Response Example:

1. Apple slices with peanut butter
2. Carrot sticks with hummus
3. Mixed nuts and dried fruit
4. Cottage cheese with pineapple
5. Rice cakes with avocado

3. Themed Dinner Night Ideas

Prompt:
"Suggest 4 themed dinner ideas for a fun family week (e.g., taco night)."

AI Response Example:

1. **Monday**: *Italian Night* – Homemade pizzas with a salad.
2. **Tuesday**: *Taco Tuesday* – Beef, chicken, or veggie tacos with toppings.

3. **Wednesday**: *Asian Night* – Chicken stir-fry with rice or noodles.
4. **Thursday**: *Mediterranean Night* – Grilled chicken or falafel with pita and tzatziki.

Tips for Effective Recipe and Meal Planning Prompts

1. **Specify Dietary Preferences**: Mention if you need vegetarian, vegan, gluten-free, or low-carb options.
2. **Include Time Constraints**: Let AI know if you need quick recipes (e.g., under 30 minutes).
3. **Identify Ingredients**: Specify any ingredients you have on hand or want to use up.
4. **Set a Theme**: Themes (e.g., "comfort food," "healthy meals," or "international cuisine") help the AI tailor ideas.

Detailed Prompt Example:
"Create a 5-day gluten-free meal plan with easy recipes, each taking under 30 minutes to cook."

By using these prompts, you can simplify your meal planning, discover new recipes, and make cooking enjoyable and stress-free. In the next chapter, we'll explore how AI can assist with time management and productivity!

Chapter 10: Prompts for Time Management and Productivity

Time management is essential for maintaining balance and getting things done, whether you're managing work, school, childcare, or personal projects. By using AI to generate customized to-do lists, schedules, and productivity strategies, you can stay organized and reduce stress. This chapter provides practical prompts to help you create daily plans and time-blocking schedules that fit your busy lifestyle.

Daily Organization

Creating structure in your day helps ensure tasks get done efficiently while allowing time for self-care and relaxation. AI can generate clear and adaptable daily plans tailored to your needs.

1. To-Do List

A well-organized to-do list can make a busy day feel manageable by breaking tasks down into clear, actionable steps.

Prompt Example:
"Create a daily to-do list for a busy mom juggling work and childcare."

AI Response Example:

Daily To-Do List for a Busy Mom

Morning:

- [7:00 AM] Wake up and prepare breakfast for the family.
- [7:30 AM] Get the kids ready for school (pack lunches, check backpacks).
- [8:00 AM] Drop the kids off at school.
- [8:30 AM] Quick 15-minute workout or stretch session.

Work Hours:

- [9:00 AM] Check and respond to urgent emails.
- [10:00 AM] Focused work session: Complete priority work tasks.
- [12:00 PM] Lunch break (prepare a healthy meal).

- [12:30 PM] Second focused work session: Attend meetings or complete assignments.

Afternoon:

- [3:00 PM] Pick up kids from school.
- [3:30 PM] Help kids with homework and school projects.
- [4:30 PM] Prep dinner while kids have playtime or screen time.

Evening:

- [5:30 PM] Family dinner.
- [6:00 PM] Clean up the kitchen.
- [6:30 PM] Quality time with the kids (play games, read books).
- [7:30 PM] Kids' bedtime routine (bath, pajamas, bedtime story).

Night:

- [8:00 PM] Wind down (relax, read, or catch up on a favorite show).
- [9:00 PM] Quick review of tomorrow's schedule and prep for the day ahead.
- [9:30 PM] Bedtime.

2. Time-Blocking Schedule

Time-blocking is a productivity technique where you divide your day into blocks of time dedicated to specific tasks. This method helps you stay focused, reduces procrastination, and ensures you balance priorities like work, study, and exercise.

Prompt Example:
"Design a time-blocking schedule to balance study, work, and exercise."

AI Response Example:

Time-Blocking Schedule for Balance

Time	Activity
6:30 AM	Wake up, morning stretch/yoga (15 minutes)
7:00 AM	Breakfast and morning routine
8:00 AM	Work block: Focus on priority tasks
10:00 AM	Short break (15 minutes)
10:15 AM	Work block: Respond to emails, attend meetings
12:00 PM	Lunch break

12:30 PM	Study block: Review notes or complete assignments
2:00 PM	Short break (15 minutes)
2:15 PM	Work block: Finish work tasks or projects
4:00 PM	Exercise: 30-minute workout (run, gym, or home workout)
4:30 PM	Shower and wind down
5:00 PM	Free time, hobbies, or relax
6:00 PM	Dinner
7:00 PM	Study or review for an hour
8:00 PM	Relax, family time, or leisure
9:30 PM	Plan for the next day, bedtime routine

Tips for Effective Time-Blocking:

1. **Group Similar Tasks**: Combine related tasks (e.g., emails and calls) into the same block.
2. **Include Breaks**: Short breaks between blocks help maintain energy and focus.
3. **Stay Flexible**: Life happens! Adjust blocks as needed without guilt.

4. **Use Tools**: Apps like Google Calendar, Trello, or Todoist can help organize your blocks.

Other Useful Time Management Prompts

1. Weekly Planner

Prompt:
"Create a weekly planner for a college student balancing classes, part-time work, and social activities."

2. Prioritization Plan

Prompt:
"Suggest a way to prioritize daily tasks when everything feels urgent."

AI Response Example:

1. **Urgent & Important**: Do these first.
2. **Important but Not Urgent**: Schedule these.
3. **Urgent but Not Important**: Delegate if possible.
4. **Not Urgent & Not Important**: Consider eliminating or postponing.

3. Productivity Tips for Focus

Prompt:
"Give me 5 productivity tips to stay focused while working from home."

AI Response Example:

1. **Create a Dedicated Workspace**: Separate work from personal spaces.
2. **Use the Pomodoro Technique**: Work for 25 minutes, then take a 5-minute break.
3. **Set Clear Goals for the Day**: Know what you want to accomplish.
4. **Limit Distractions**: Turn off notifications and set phone boundaries.
5. **Schedule Breaks**: Regular breaks help maintain energy and avoid burnout.

Tips for Effective Time Management Prompts

1. **Be Specific**: Include details like your roles, responsibilities, and time constraints.
2. **Set Goals**: Identify what you want to achieve (e.g., balance, focus, productivity).

3. **Include Time Limits**: Specify how long you can dedicate to each task.
4. **Prioritize Tasks**: Mention what's most important to you so the AI can create a plan around your priorities.

Example of a Detailed Prompt:
"Create a time-blocking schedule for a freelancer who works 6 hours a day, exercises for 1 hour, and spends 2 hours on personal development."

By using these AI-generated prompts, you can organize your time, boost productivity, and balance work, study, and self-care effectively. In the next chapter, we'll explore advanced prompting tips to further enhance your AI-assisted tasks!

Chapter 11: Advanced Prompting Tips

Now that you've mastered the basics of crafting effective prompts, it's time to explore advanced prompting techniques. These methods can help you get more precise, detailed, and useful responses from AI. By incorporating strategies like **Chain of Thought** and **Role-Playing**, you can break down complex tasks, generate specialized content, and unlock the full potential of AI for your needs.

1. Chain of Thought: Step-by-Step Questioning

What is Chain of Thought?

Chain of Thought prompting helps you break down a complex task or problem into a series of step-by-step questions. Instead of asking for a complete solution all at once, you guide the AI through the task by addressing each part in sequence.

Why Use Chain of Thought?

- **Clarity**: Helps the AI provide more detailed and accurate responses.
- **Depth**: Allows for more comprehensive answers by addressing each step.
- **Problem-Solving**: Effective for tasks that involve multiple components, like research, calculations, or planning.

Example Prompt Using Chain of Thought

Task: *Create a detailed plan for starting a side business.*

1. **Step 1**: *"What are some low-cost business ideas that can be started from home?"*
2. **Step 2**: *"For the business idea of selling handmade candles, what materials and supplies are needed?"*
3. **Step 3**: *"What are the key steps to creating an online store for handmade candles?"*
4. **Step 4**: *"How can I market handmade candles on social media to attract customers?"*

Why This Works:
By breaking down the task into individual steps, the AI can provide focused and actionable advice for each part, leading to a more thorough and useful overall plan.

2. Role-Playing: Specialized Responses

What is Role-Playing?

Role-Playing prompts instruct the AI to take on a specific persona or role. This technique helps the AI provide more specialized, context-specific, and insightful responses tailored to the scenario you need.

Why Use Role-Playing?

- **Expert Advice**: Receive responses that simulate expertise in a specific field.
- **Tone and Perspective**: Get content that matches the tone, language, and approach of the role you specify.
- **Creativity**: Useful for generating ideas, dialogue, or scenarios where different perspectives are needed.

Example Role-Playing Prompts

1. **Financial Advisor**:
   Prompt: *"Act as a financial advisor and provide a simple investment strategy for someone in their 30s with $1,000 to invest."*
   AI Response Example:
   "As your financial advisor, I'd recommend starting with a diversified, low-risk approach. Consider putting $700 into a broad-market ETF like the S&P 500 and $300 into

a bond ETF for stability. This combination balances growth and security."

2. **Fitness Coach**:
   Prompt: "Act as a fitness coach and design a 4-week workout plan for a beginner who wants to get fit at home."
   AI Response Example:
   "Week 1: Focus on building a foundation. Do 3 days of 20-minute workouts that include bodyweight exercises like squats, push-ups, and lunges..."

3. **Customer Service Representative**:
   Prompt: "Act as a customer service representative responding to a complaint about a delayed order."
   AI Response Example:
   "Dear [Customer's Name], I'm sincerely sorry for the delay in your order. We understand how important it is to receive your items on time and apologize for the inconvenience..."

4. **Travel Planner**:
   Prompt: "Act as a travel planner and create a 5-day itinerary for a trip to Paris."
   AI Response Example:
   "Day 1: Explore the Eiffel Tower, walk along the Seine River, and have dinner at a traditional French bistro..."

Combining Chain of Thought and Role-Playing

You can also combine **Chain of Thought** and **Role-Playing** techniques for even more powerful prompting.

Example Combined Prompt

Task: *Create a detailed budget plan for a family of four.*

Prompt:

1. *"Act as a financial advisor. What are the key categories a family of four should include in their monthly budget?"*
2. *"Now, break down each category with recommended percentages of income for housing, food, transportation, savings, and entertainment."*
3. *"Given a monthly income of $5,000, how would you allocate funds to each category?"*

Why This Works:

- The **Role-Playing** technique ensures the response comes from a financial expert's perspective.
- The **Chain of Thought** structure breaks the task into logical steps, leading to a more thorough and detailed budget plan.

Other Advanced Prompting Techniques

1. Specify Output Format

Ask the AI to structure the response in a particular format like a **bullet list**, **step-by-step guide**, **table**, or **essay**.

Prompt Example:
"Explain the water cycle in a step-by-step guide suitable for a 6th-grade science class."

2. Provide Constraints or Limits

Set constraints like word count, tone, or complexity level to get the most relevant output.

Prompt Example:
"Summarize the benefits of exercise in under 100 words."

3. Use Examples in Your Prompts

Include examples in your prompt to clarify what you want.

Prompt Example:
"Create a motivational quote similar to 'Believe you can, and you're halfway there.'"

Tips for Using Advanced Prompts Effectively

1. **Be Clear and Detailed**: The more precise your prompt, the better the AI's output.
2. **Combine Techniques**: Use multiple techniques (e.g., Role-Playing + Chain of Thought) for complex tasks.
3. **Refine and Iterate**: If the AI's first response isn't perfect, adjust your prompt and try again.
4. **Set Boundaries**: Include constraints to keep responses on track (e.g., "Explain in two paragraphs" or "List five points").

By mastering these advanced prompting techniques, you can unlock even greater potential from AI, making it a more versatile tool for solving complex problems, generating specialized content, and enhancing productivity.

In the next chapter, we'll wrap things up with answers to frequently asked questions and common pitfalls to avoid when using AI!

Chapter 12: FAQs and Common Pitfalls

Using AI for everyday tasks and projects can be incredibly helpful, but it's not without challenges. Sometimes the AI might not give you the response you expect, or you may wonder about the limits of AI's capabilities. In this chapter, we'll address frequently asked questions and highlight some common pitfalls to help you use AI effectively and avoid frustration.

Common Questions

1. "Why didn't the AI understand my prompt?"

Sometimes the AI response isn't what you expected because the prompt was too vague or lacked context. The AI relies on the details you provide to generate accurate and relevant responses.

Solution:

- **Add More Context**: Provide background information or specifics about the task.
- **Be Specific**: Clearly outline what you want, including the tone, format, or any examples.
- **Break It Down**: If the task is complex, use step-by-step or Chain of Thought prompting.

Example:

- ✗ *"Write a report about marketing."*
- ■ *"Write a 500-word report on digital marketing strategies for small businesses, focusing on social media platforms like Instagram and Facebook."*

---

2. "Can I rely on AI for everything?"

No, AI is a **tool**—it's not a replacement for human judgment, creativity, or critical thinking. While AI can generate helpful content and ideas, it still has limitations.

Answer:

- **Fact-Checking**: AI can sometimes provide incorrect or outdated information. Always verify critical facts.
- **Human Touch**: Tasks requiring emotional intelligence, nuanced judgment, or creativity often need a human touch.

- **Ethical Considerations**: Be mindful of privacy, attribution, and responsible AI use.

Use AI to **assist** you, not to make all the decisions for you.

---

3. "How can I get the AI to generate more creative responses?"

If AI responses feel generic or uninspired, your prompt may need a creative boost.

Solution:

- **Add Constraints**: Ask the AI to respond in a particular style, tone, or format.
- **Use Role-Playing**: Ask the AI to "Act as…" a specific character or professional.
- **Give Examples**: Provide a sample or describe the kind of creativity you're looking for.

Example:

- ✗ "Write a story about a dog."
- ■ "Write a whimsical children's story about a talking dog who wants to become a chef in Paris."

---

4. "Why is the AI response too long or too short?"

Sometimes AI may provide more detail than you need or not enough.

Solution:

- **Set Clear Limits**: Specify word count, sentence length, or detail level.
- **Ask for Summaries**: If the output is too long, request a condensed version.
- **Request More Detail**: If the response is too short, ask the AI to expand on specific points.

Example:

- ✗ *"Explain photosynthesis."*
- ■ *"Explain photosynthesis in 2-3 concise paragraphs suitable for a 5th-grade science student."*

---

5. "What if I don't know what to ask?"

Sometimes you might struggle with how to phrase your prompt.

Solution:

- **Start Broad**: Ask general questions and refine the prompt based on the AI's response.
- **Use Templates**: Follow prompt templates or structures provided in this book.
- **Ask for Help**: Use prompts like, *"What's a good way to start a blog post about mindfulness?"*

Common Pitfalls and How to Avoid Them

1. Being Too Vague

Pitfall: Providing a general or unclear prompt.

Example:

- *"Write something about finance."*

Solution: Add context, specify the audience, and set the tone.

Improved Prompt:

- *"Write a beginner-friendly guide explaining the basics of saving and investing for young professionals."*

2. Ignoring Fact-Checking

Pitfall: Assuming everything the AI generates is accurate.

Solution: Always verify facts, especially for educational, professional, or legal content. Use reputable sources to confirm AI-generated information.

---

3. Overloading the Prompt

Pitfall: Cramming too many requests into one prompt.

Example:

- *"Write an email about a delayed order, suggest three solutions, and also include a product discount code."*

Solution: Break it into separate prompts for each part of the task.

---

4. Forgetting Tone and Audience

Pitfall: Not specifying who the content is for or the tone you want.

Example:

- *"Write a social media post about our new product."*

Solution: Include details about your audience and the tone.

Improved Prompt:

- *"Write a friendly and engaging Instagram post announcing our new eco-friendly water bottle to young adults."*

---

5. Relying Too Heavily on AI

Pitfall: Using AI without adding your own insights or personalization.

Solution: Use AI as a starting point. Add your personal touch, voice, or additional context to make the content uniquely yours.

Quick Recap of Tips

- **Add Context**: Provide background information and specific details.
- **Specify Output**: Clarify format, tone, and length.
- **Refine and Iterate**: Adjust your prompts based on the AI's response.
- **Verify Information**: Don't assume everything is accurate—always double-check.
- **Use AI as a Tool**: Combine AI's efficiency with your creativity and judgment.

By keeping these FAQs and pitfalls in mind, you'll be able to use AI more effectively, avoid common mistakes, and get the most out of your AI-assisted tasks. In the next and final chapter, we'll discuss how to continue your AI journey and explore new ways to integrate AI into your life.

Chapter 13: Conclusion and Next Steps

Congratulations! You've reached the final chapter of this guide. By now, you've learned how to use AI prompts effectively across various aspects of daily life—from writing emails and managing personal finances to crafting social media posts, planning meals, and boosting productivity. You've also explored advanced techniques like **Chain of Thought** and **Role-Playing** to take your AI interactions to the next level.

This is just the beginning of your AI journey. The more you experiment and refine your prompts, the better your results will be. The possibilities with AI are constantly expanding, and your ability to harness its potential will only grow with practice.

Key Takeaways

1. **Start with Clear, Specific Prompts**: The more detail you provide, the better the AI can understand and meet your needs.

2. **Iterate and Refine**: Don't be afraid to tweak your prompts. Each adjustment helps you learn what works best.
3. **Use Context and Tone**: Providing background information and specifying tone can dramatically improve the relevance and quality of AI responses.
4. **Stay Ethical and Responsible**: Always verify facts, respect privacy, and give credit where it's due.
5. **Leverage Advanced Techniques**: Use strategies like **Chain of Thought** and **Role-Playing** to tackle more complex tasks effectively.

Keep Experimenting and Learning

AI is a tool that rewards creativity and curiosity. Here are a few ways you can continue to grow your skills:

1. **Explore New Use Cases**: Think beyond the examples in this book. How else can AI assist you? Maybe in planning trips, brainstorming business ideas, or learning new skills.
2. **Try Different AI Tools**: Experiment with various AI platforms like ChatGPT, Google Gemini, or specialized AI tools for tasks like design, data analysis, or language translation.

3. **Join AI Communities**: Participate in online forums, social media groups, or AI workshops to exchange ideas and learn from others.
4. **Stay Updated**: AI is evolving rapidly. Keep up with new features, tools, and best practices to stay ahead of the curve.
5. **Teach Others**: Share what you've learned with friends, family, or colleagues. Helping others use AI effectively reinforces your own skills.

The Future of AI in Daily Life

As AI technology continues to improve, it will become an even more integral part of our everyday lives. From smart assistants in our homes to AI-driven tools in the workplace, AI is here to make tasks more efficient and life more manageable. The key is to approach AI with a sense of wonder, responsibility, and adaptability.

By understanding how to craft effective prompts, you're not just using AI—you're partnering with it to achieve your goals, spark creativity, and enhance productivity.

Your Next Steps

1. **Pick a Task**: Choose one task from your daily life and use an AI prompt to help you complete it.
2. **Refine and Improve**: Review the AI's response and refine your prompt for better results.
3. **Set a Challenge**: Challenge yourself to use AI for a new task each week.
4. **Reflect**: Take note of what works and what doesn't. Keep a record of your best prompts for future use.

Final Thought

The power of AI is in your hands. The more you experiment and integrate AI into your routine, the more you'll realize how much it can simplify, enhance, and inspire your daily life.

You've got the tools, the knowledge, and the creativity—now go out there and see what amazing things you can accomplish with AI!

Thank you for joining me on this journey. Happy prompting!